THIS BO
BELONG

Name: Age:

Favourite player:

2021/2022

My Predictions...   Actual...

The Rams' final position:

The Rams' top scorer:

Sky Bet EFL Championship Winners:

Sky Bet EFL Championship top scorer:

FA Cup winners:

Carabao Cup Winners:

Contributors: Peter Rogers

A TWOCAN PUBLICATION

©2021. Published by twocan under licence from Derby County Football Club.

Every effort has been made to ensure the accuracy of information within this publication but the publishers cannot be held responsible for any errors or omissions. Views expressed are those of the authors and do not necessarily represent those of the publishers or the football club. All rights reserved.

ISBN: 978-1-913362-94-2

PICTURE CREDITS: Action Images, Alamy, Andy Clarke, Derby County Football Club, Press Association.

£9

CONTENTS

01 DAVID MARSHALL

POSITION: Goalkeeper

DOB: 05/03/1985

COUNTRY: Scotland

Scotland international goalkeeper David Marshall brings a vast wealth of experience to the Derby County goalkeeping department.

The former Celtic, Norwich, Cardiff and Hull stopper is a commanding character whose presence certainly provides confidence to those playing in front of him. He made 33 appearances for the Rams in 2020/21 before representing his country in the summer's UEFA European Championships.

02 NATHAN BYRNE

POSITION: Defender

DOB: 05/06/1992

COUNTRY: England

Following his arrival at Pride Park ahead of the 2020/21 season, 29-year-old Nathan Byrne wasted little time in make the Rams' right-back spot his own.

The Tottenham Hotspur trainee, who joined Derby from Wigan Athletic, featured in 41 of the Rams' 46 Championship matches last season and is sure to be another key performer for Wayne Rooney's side again in 2021/22.

SQUAD
2021/22

03 CRAIG FORSYTH

POSITION: Defender

DOB: 24/02/1989

COUNTRY: Scotland

Among the current squad, left-sided defender Craig Forsyth is Derby County's longest-serving player and the 2021/22 campaign will be his ninth full season at Pride Park.

With the flexibility of being able to play at left-back or as a centre-half, the Scottish international is always comfortable in possession and likes to get forward and support attacks when playing at left-back.

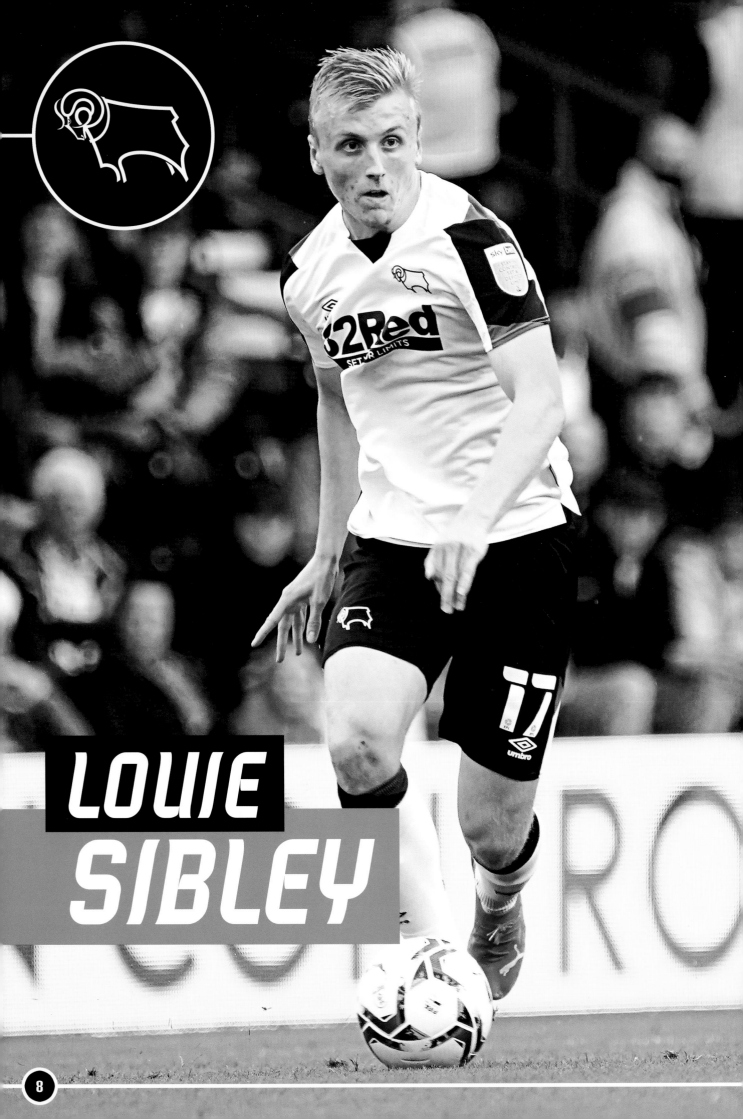

LOUIE
SIBLEY

The side-foot pass is one of the most accurate passing techniques over shorter distances. The ability to find one of your teammates with a pass, even when under severe pressure, and retain possession of the ball is an essential factor in the way the game is played today.

SIDE-FOOT PASS

SOCCER SKILLS

EXERCISE ONE

Set up a 10 x 10m grid. In one corner there are two players and on each of the other three corners there is one player.

Player A starts with the ball. Each player must pass the ball round the square in sequence then follow their pass. A passes to B then runs after his pass and takes up B's starting position. B passes to C and follows his pass to take C's position, and so on. All of the players must control the ball then pass it with the inside of their foot.

Key Factors

1. Non-kicking foot alongside the ball.
2. Pass with the inside of the foot.
3. Strike through the middle of the ball.
4. Keep your eyes on the ball and your head steady.

EXERCISE TWO

The set up is the same as exercise one.

In this exercise the players pass the ball in sequence, A through to D, but do not follow their pass, remaining stationary.

As soon as A plays the first pass, E sets off racing around the outside of the starting point. The players must pass the ball as quickly and accurately as possible while under pressure from E, who cannot tackle but is effectively racing the ball round the square.

The same key factors apply in this exercise as in the first, but the players are required to be able to pass the ball accurately while under pressure.

Any team who can retain possession through good accurate passing will always make it very difficult for the opposition. The side-foot pass is one of the most accurate passing techniques.

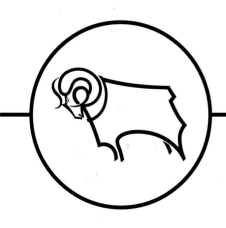

Derby County completed the sensational signing of England goalkeeper Peter Shilton from Southampton in the summer of 1987 following the club's back-to-back promotion success which saw the Rams back in the top flight.

Shilton arrived at the Baseball Ground firmly acknowledged as the country's top stopper and had represented England in the 1986 World Cup finals in Mexico.

A vastly-experienced player who needed no introduction to his new teammates, the signing of Shilton was seen as a major statement that Derby County were heading back to the big time and were in the First Division to compete, not just make up the numbers.

RAMS HEROES

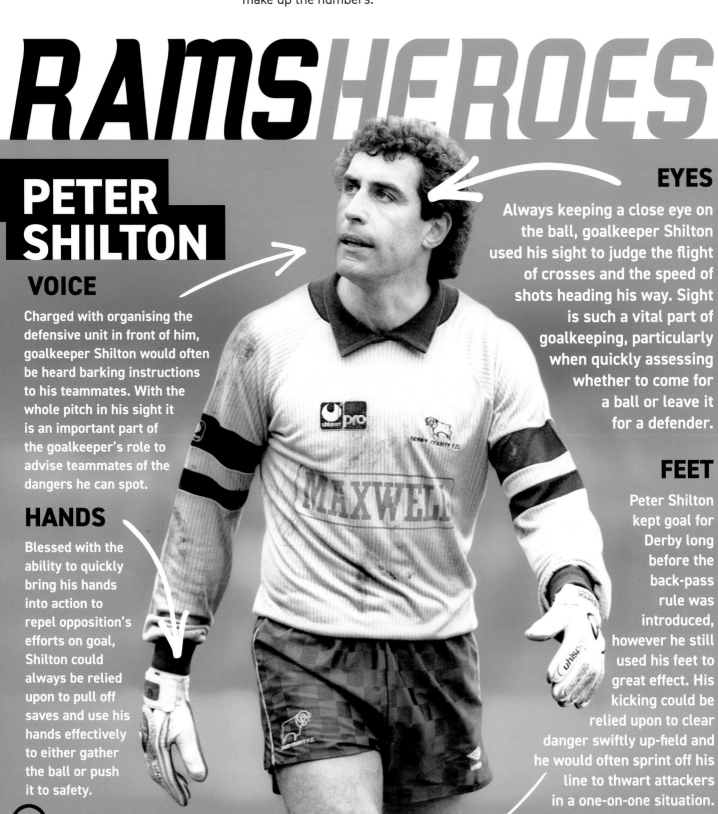

PETER SHILTON

VOICE

Charged with organising the defensive unit in front of him, goalkeeper Shilton would often be heard barking instructions to his teammates. With the whole pitch in his sight it is an important part of the goalkeeper's role to advise teammates of the dangers he can spot.

HANDS

Blessed with the ability to quickly bring his hands into action to repel opposition's efforts on goal, Shilton could always be relied upon to pull off saves and use his hands effectively to either gather the ball or push it to safety.

EYES

Always keeping a close eye on the ball, goalkeeper Shilton used his sight to judge the flight of crosses and the speed of shots heading his way. Sight is such a vital part of goalkeeping, particularly when quickly assessing whether to come for a ball or leave it for a defender.

FEET

Peter Shilton kept goal for Derby long before the back-pass rule was introduced, however he still used his feet to great effect. His kicking could be relied upon to clear danger swiftly up-field and he would often sprint off his line to thwart attackers in a one-on-one situation.

ALL OF THESE FOOTY TERMS ARE HIDDEN IN THE GRID, EXCEPT FOR ONE... CAN YOU WORK OUT WHICH ONE?

```
A G F G O L D E N G O A L A A V C U R B
O C L E A N S H E E T N T X O A S A E V
D R I B B L I N G A Y H B L U C A T M I
E B P H R N R U T F F Y U R C V N S O F
A F F H I T T H E W O O D W O R K M J G
D I L C E N S X D T V R C G R G E O T S
B M A D J P Z E U I W J F N E A D E Z M
A R P K U L I E F S B M A M P I K O S R
L Q A T A T M S D O E M T R P J P Q P A
L Y V C P O A G O I D U A A I Y T N B I
S I W U E T G T A R N V B T K A H V W N
P R C L I N I C A L F I N I S H E R N B
E R Z N S T C H X M A M A M I E N L A O
C Q E H C N S H Y O S U J G L T U E M W
I O A F O S P T E W R O D B Z A M X T K
A J I N F F O X I N T H E B O X B F E I
L K A D E A N T Y V N R K B S Q I C G C
I M G F M U G I A N T K I L L I N G R K
S X P B U H E L G L O R T N O C L L A B
T H E B E A U T I F U L G A M E S P T T
```

SOCCERSEARCH

Ball Control	Clinical Finisher	Flip Flap	Hard Man	Rainbow Kick
Bicycle Kick	Cruyff Turn	Fox in the Box	Hit the Woodwork	Skipper
Boot it	Cup-tied	Gaffer	Magic Sponge	Target Man
Brace	Dead-ball Specialist	Giant-killing	Man On	The Beautiful Game
Clean Sheet	Dribbling	Golden Goal	Nutmeg	Treble

ANSWERS ON PAGE 62

11

04 GRAEME SHINNIE

POSITION: Midfielder

DOB: 04/08/1991

COUNTRY: Scotland

Scotland international Graeme Shinnie really became the heartbeat of the Rams' midfield in 2020/21 making 43 appearances in all competitions for the club.

The former Aberdeen man won many plaudits for his tenacious ball-winning play and netted three Championship goals in 2020/21 - two from the penalty spot in victories over Birmingham City and Luton Town and one from open play against promotion-chasing Bournemouth.

05 KRYSTIAN BIELIK

POSITION: Midfielder

DOB: 04/01/1998

COUNTRY: Poland

Midfielder Krystian Bielik joined Derby County from Arsenal in August 2019 and made a positive impression during his 21 appearances for the club in 2019/20.

Sadly a knee injury suffered in January 2020 then ruled the Polish international out for ten months. He returned to the side midway through the 2020/21 campaign and his performances won rave reviews. The 23-year-old will be hopeful of an injury-free 2021/22 season and the chance to really make his mark at Pride Park.

SQUAD
2021/22

06 PHIL JAGIELKA

POSITION: Defender

DOB: 17/08/1982

COUNTRY: England

With the 2021/22 Championship season already underway, the Rams bolstered their defensive options when they agreed a short-term contract with former England international defender Phil Jagielka.

The highly-experienced central defender put pen to paper on a deal with Derby county on his 39th birthday and made his debut the following day in a 1-0 victory away to Hull City. With vast Premier League and international experience to call upon, Jagielka's presence will certainly be of great benefit to a youthful Rams squad.

There are five Rammies hiding in the crowd as Derby County return home with the FA Cup following their victory over Charlton Athletic in the final at Wembley in 1946.

Can you find Rammie?

CLASSIC FANTASTIC

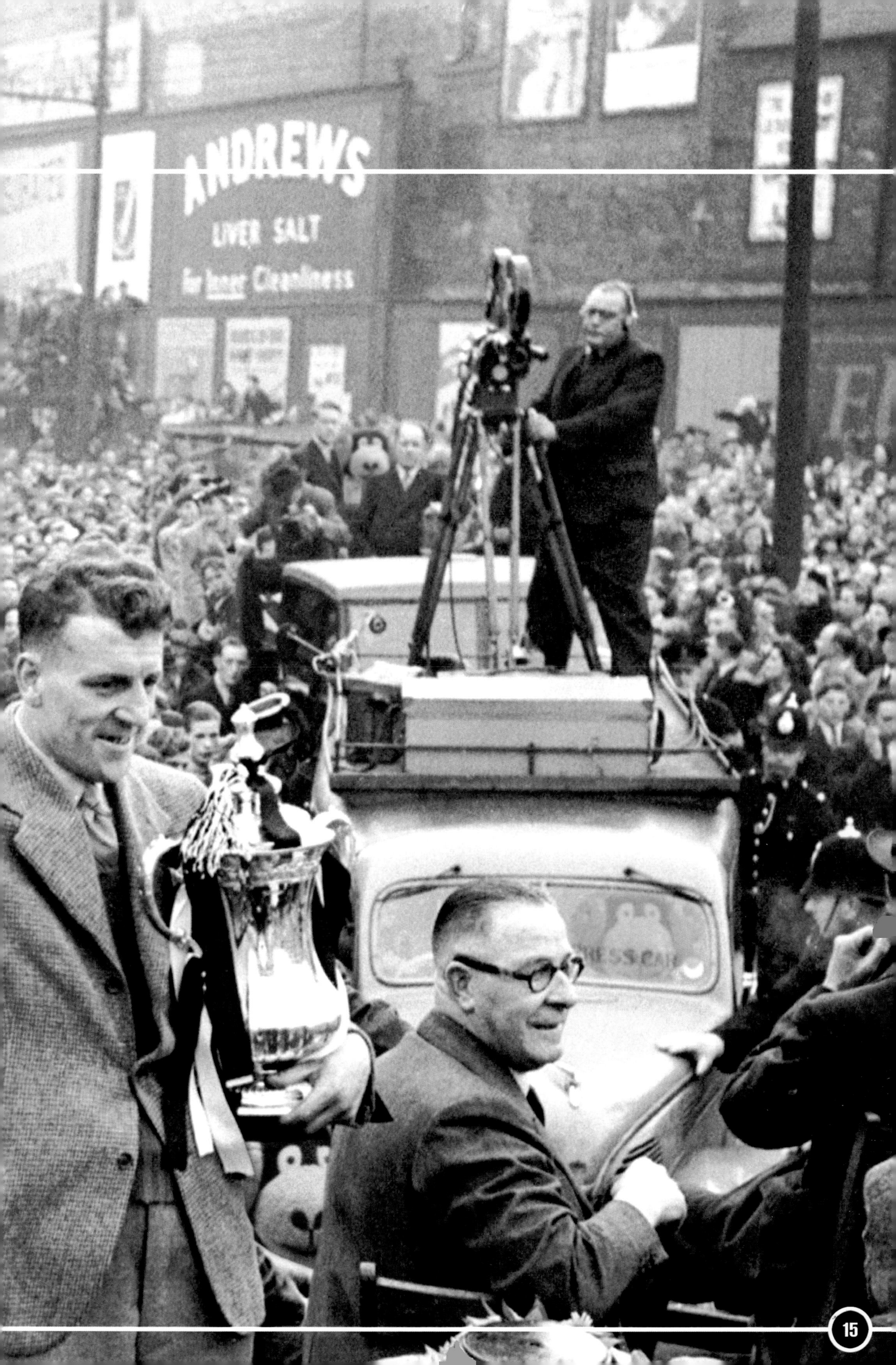
ANDREWS
LIVER SALT
for Inner Cleanliness

DESIGN A KIT

Have a go at creating next season's home kit for the Rams!

CURTIS
DAVIES

The Rams' proud white shirts have been a long-held tradition at the club.

However, a great deal of excitement and anticipation still surrounds the launch of every new Derby County kit.

Each and every playing strip forms its own part of the Rams' proud history and supporters young and old will all have their own favourites. Let's take a look back at four of the best...

1988/89

Following the club's promotion back to the First Division in 1987, the Rams then teamed up with kit supplier Umbro who produced a new-look strip for the top flight.

Umbro introduced a trendy round neck buttoned collar and added a diamond-effect pattern to the white shirt. The shirts had a dark blue collar and a thin line of dark blue piping on the sleeves which ran down to meet a dark blue cuff. The club crest and Umbro branding sat above the sponsor's logo in the centre of the shirt.

The dark blue shorts had a chequered effect and a thin white trim on the sides, they also carried the club crest and manufacturer's branding. A dark blue sock was topped with a white band and the Umbro logo on the shin pad area.

DRESSED TO IMPRESS

Derby enjoyed an excellent top-flight campaign wearing this kit in 1988/89 and ended the season in fifth place.

Always a tough nut to crack at the Baseball Ground, the Rams also enjoyed impressive away wins at White Hart Lane, Old Trafford and Highbury to help them amass a 58-point finish.

HE WORE IT WELL

The Rams smashed their record transfer fee in October 1988 when Wales international Dean Saunders became the club's first £1M player.

A prolific scorer with Oxford United, Saunders hit the ground running in a Derby shirt, netting six times in his first five games. His signing was an important factor in the club's rise up the First Division table.

Not only did sports manufacturer Puma become the club's kit provider in 1995/96 but they also became club sponsor too.

A white shirt with an attractive black, striped pattern and yellow piping on the sleeve and shoulder area was capped off by a v-neck black collar with white and yellow trim. Both the club crest and sponsor's logo were positioned in the centre of the shirt.

The pattern from the shirt was repeated on the sides of the black shorts which also carried the club crest and Puma logo. The white socks were topped with yellow and black banding. The Puma logo and club name was also on the front of the socks.

DRESSED TO IMPRESS

Under the management of Jim Smith, Derby County capped off an exciting 1995/96 season as they reached the holy grail of the Premier League.

After suffering Play-Off heartbreak two seasons earlier, the Rams held off the challenge of Crystal Palace to secure the second automatic promotion place behind champions Sunderland.

HE WORE IT WELL

Dutch midfielder Robin Van der Laan played a key role in the Rams' 1995/96 promotion-winning season and netted the all-important goal that secured promotion.

With Derby's destiny in their own hands in their final home game of the season, victory over fellow promotion hopefuls Crystal Palace would see Jim Smith's side up with a game to spare. The match was all square at 1-1 at the break and Van der Laan then headed home what proved to be the promotion winning goal after 66 minutes to seal the points needed.

1995/96

ALL KITTED OUT

07 KAMIL JOZWIAK

POSITION: Forward

DOB: 22/04/1998

COUNTRY: Poland

The 2020/21 campaign will be Polish winger Kamil Jozwiak's second full season in the English game having joined Derby County from Lech Poznan in September 2020.

The 23-year-old featured in 41 Championship games last season and his form won him a place in his country's squad for the Euro 2020 finals where he started all three of Poland's group games.

08 MAX BIRD

POSITION: Midfielder

DOB: 18/09/2000

COUNTRY: England

Midfielder Max Bird has progressed through the Rams' successful youth Academy to really make his mark on the first-team scene.

Bird made his first-team debut back in September 2017 in an EFL Cup tie and established himself in the side in the second half of the 2019/20 season. He made 34 appearances for the club in 2020/21 and is sure to be a player that fans will be excited to see in 2021/22.

SQUAD
2021/22

09 SAM BALDOCK

POSITION: Forward

DOB: 15/03/1989

COUNTRY: England

Forward Sam Baldock enjoyed a memorable Derby County debut by scoring the only goal of the game to give the Rams all three points from their Championship trip to Hull City in August 2021.

An experienced campaigner at Championship level, Baldock trained with the Rams throughout the summer of 2021 as a free agent and agreed an initial short-term deal at Pride Park that runs until January 2022.

Keeping fit and healthy is vital for all of us. So if you play footy for the school team or your local club, being fit and ready for action is sure to help you enjoy the game and perform to your very best.

For the players at Derby County, showing peak levels of fitness is essential if they want to feature in Wayne Rooney's team. Before anyone can think of pulling on the famous white shirt and taking to the pitch at Pride Park on a Saturday afternoon, they will have had to perform well in training at Moor Farm and to have shown the manager, his coaches and fitness staff that they are fully fit and ready for the physical challenges that await them on a matchday.

Regardless of whether training takes place at the training ground or at the stadium, the players' fitness remains an all-important factor.

Of course, time spent working on training drills and playing small-sided games will help a player's fitness, but there is lots of work undertaken just to ensure maximum levels of fitness are reached. Away from the training pitches the professional players will spend a great deal of time in the gymnasium partaking in their own personal workouts. Bikes, treadmills and weights will all form part of helping the players reach and maintain a top level of fitness.

Over the course of a week the players will take part in many warm-up and aerobic sessions and even complete yoga and pilates classes to help with core strength and general fitness. The strength and conditioning coaches at the club work tirelessly to do all they can to make sure that the Derby County players you see in action on a matchday really are fighting fit for footy!

GET FIT FOR FOOTY

RAVEL
MORRISON

It has been said that dribbling is a dying art. The pace of the modern game makes it more difficult, but there are players about, even in today's lightning fast conditions, who have the confidence to keep hold of the ball and take on defenders.

DRIBBLING

SOCCERSKILLS

EXERCISE ONE

As a warm-up exercise, players A and B each dribble a ball around a 20 x 10m grid, avoiding each other, but staying within the grid boundary lines.

They progress to a 'cat and mouse' race between the corners - the player with the most visits to each corner wins the race. One of the main problems in this exercise is avoiding the other player, and their ball.

EXERCISE TWO

Now for a more realistic exercise. Six players are used as shown, with three attackers and three defenders at any one time. When play starts, the players with the ball attack any of the three opposing goals, changing their target as they choose. The defenders have, simply, to stop their opposite number from scoring, but must not interfere with any other pair.

Key Factors

1. Close control.
2. Quick change of direction.
3. Acceleration away from defender.
4. Feints, to wrong-foot defender.
5. Head up to see the whole picture.

When the defenders win possession, they become the attackers, and go for goal themselves. This can be a very enjoyable practice, but also quite tiring.

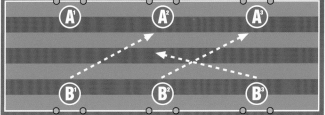

1
ANSWER

2
ANSWER

3
ANSWER

4
ANSWER

5
ANSWER

GUESS

THE CLUB

6 ANSWER

7 ANSWER

8 ANSWER

9 ANSWER

10 ANSWER

Each football holds the clues to the identity of a Premier League or EFL club, how quickly can you solve them?

ANSWERS ON PAGE 62

SQUAD
2021/22

10 TOM LAWRENCE

POSITION: Midfielder

DOB: 13/01/1994

COUNTRY: Wales

A full Wales international, midfielder Tom Lawrence joined the Rams from Midlands rivals Leicester City in August 2017. He was handed the club captaincy ahead of the 2021/22 campaign which will be his fifth season at Pride Park.

A quality goalscoring performer at Championship level, Lawrence loves to break forward from wide or central areas and shoot for goal. He also has great awareness of those around him and is a capable provider of assists for teammates.

11 RAVEL MORRISON

POSITION: Midfielder

DOB: 02/02/1993

COUNTRY: Jamaica

On the eve of the new 2021/22 Championship season Derby County completed the signing of attacking midfielder Ravel Morrison.

The 28-year-old trained with the Rams during pre-season and impressed in a number of the friendly fixtures. The former Manchester United and West Ham man had been capped by Jamaica at international level on three occasions and brings real attacking flair to the Derby squad.

13 COLIN KAZIM-RICHARDS

POSITION: Striker

DOB: 26/08/1986

COUNTRY: Turkey

Powerful striker Colin Kazim-Richards enjoyed an impressive first season at Pride Park having joined the Rams in October 2020.

The Turkish international repaid the faith that manager Wayne Rooney placed in him by topping the club's scoring charts in 2020/21 with eight Championship goals from 30 league starts in a Derby shirt. His excellent form won him a contract extension for the 2021/22 campaign.

Rams boss Wayne Rooney first burst onto the Premier League scene with a sensational last-minute goal for Everton against Arsenal at Goodison Park on 19 October 2002.

That wonder-strike against the Gunners ended the Londoners' 30-match unbeaten run and introduced Wayne Rooney to the world just five days before his 17th birthday. Rooney had in fact already been on the scoresheet for the Toffees ahead of his memorable winner against Arsenal, having netted a brace in Everton's 3-0 win over Wrexham in the Second Round of the League Cup.

From the moment he let fly with that stunning strike against the Gunners, Rooney has become a household name up and down the land. A record-breaking transfer to Manchester United and a trophy-laden Old Trafford career followed.

In a truly glittering playing career, Rooney took top spot as England's leading international goalscorer with 53 goals in 120 outings for the Three Lions. He later returned to Everton, before trying his luck in the USA with DC United and then of course arrived at Pride Park in January 2020 in an exciting new role as the Rams' player/coach.

In total Rooney netted 366 career goals (313 club goals and 53 at international level), however it's goal number 366 that will live long in the memory for Rams fans and being his final career goal it is sure to have a special place in Rooney's heart too.

For a player who scored countless spectacular goals throughout his career it was only fitting that he signed off in style - and Rooney certainly did that. The venue was Norwich City's Carrow Road, the date was Saturday 3 October 2020 and although the match was played in an empty stadium due to the Covid-19 pandemic, a consolation was that the match was broadcast live on television and Rooney's sublime late winner got the audience it deserved.

The Rams had been under the cosh for large spells of the game against the team that would end up winning promotion to the Premier League as champions. After surviving a missed penalty from Norwich's Teemu Pukki earlier in the game, Rooney struck with three minutes remaining. Jason Knight was fouled by Lukas Rupp some 20 yards from goal and in Rooney, the Rams had the perfect man on the pitch to step up, break the deadlock and secure all three points for the visitors. It was a tremendous execution of a dead-ball situation as Rooney calmly curled the ball up and over the Norwich wall, past goalkeeper Tim Krul and into the top corner.

It was a goal worthy of a full stadium, a moment of sheer quality that justified winning any game and a fitting way to end a career packed with great goals.

SIGNING OFF IN STYLE

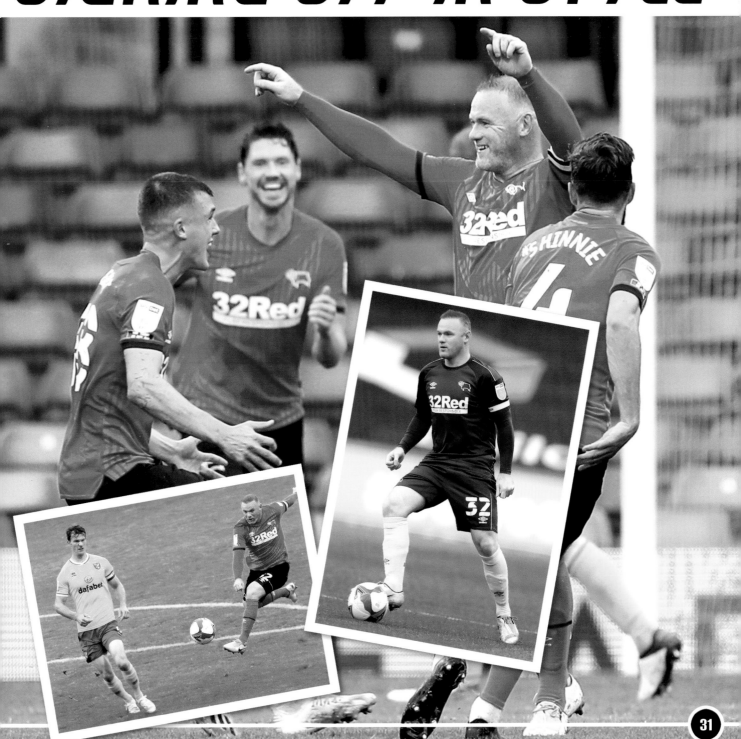

Striker Steve Howard only spent 18 months at Pride Park but became a real fans' favourite during the 2006/07 season as his goals inspired the club to Premier League promotion.

Having gained an excellent reputation at Luton Town, with 96 league goals in 212 outings for the Hatters, the powerful target-man was a player in demand when the Rams secured his services for a £1M fee.

He ended the 2006/07 season as top goalscorer with 19 goals, 16 of which came in the Championship. He is fondly remembered for his vital brace in the first leg of the Play-Off semi-final against Southampton and he played in the Play-Off final victory over West Bromwich Albion at Wembley and represented the Rams in the Premier League.

RAMS HEROES

STEVE HOWARD

HEADERS

A good number of Steve Howard's Derby goals came from headers. A real threat in the air, Howard had the power to out-jump defenders and then use his head to direct the ball past the 'keeper and into the net. Once the ball was in and around the six-yard box and in the air there was always a good chance Steve would head it home.

ENCOURAGEMENT

Often employed as the focal point of the attack, Howard could be relied upon to advise and encourage teammates to play the ball into areas where he could be most effective and cause danger to the opposition.

CHEST CONTROL

As a strong centre-forward who led the Derby attack so well, Steve was blessed with a great ability to play with his back to goal and take the ball under control on his chest. He could then hold up play while others arrived in support or lay the ball off to a teammate.

GOALS

Despite having the reputation as a target-man who caused problems in the air, Steve was pretty lethal with the ball at his feet too. Comfortable on either foot and with the ability to take shots first time - when Howard pulled the trigger he rarely missed the target.

MAX
BIRD

RECORD APPEARANCE MAKER

When it comes to appearances, no-one has made more for Derby County than striker Kevin Hector. He joined the club from Bradford Park Avenue in 1966, and went on to amass 589 appearances for the Rams.

Hector was a star performer as the Rams won the Second Division title in 1968/69 and his goals then spearheaded the club's memorable 1971/72 First Division title success. Three seasons later he added a second First Division title winners' medal to his collection as the Rams were once again English football's top dogs.

MOST INTERNATIONAL CAPS

Jamaican striker Deon Burton holds the record for winning the most international caps while playing for Derby County.

Burton appeared on 42 occasions for Jamaica while plying his trade for the Rams. He made a total of 62 appearances for his country and featured for the Reggae Boyz at the World Cup finals in France 1998. The lively frontman netted 13 goals at international level between 1997 and 2009.

TOP GOALSCORER

Record Derby County goalscorer Steve Bloomer fired home an incredible 332 goals in 525 outings for the Rams during two separate spells with the club.

His initial spell with the club spanned for 13 years from 1892 to 1905, he then spent five seasons with Middlesbrough before returning to Derby and continuing his fine goalscoring exploits for a further three seasons. A true club legend, there is a bust of him located at Pride Park in recognition of his phenomenal contribution to Derby County.

RECORD MAKERS

A selection of players, games, facts and figures which all shape the club's proud history.

RECORD ATTENDANCE

As we all know there are few better places to be than inside a packed Pride Park and helping cheer the Rams on to victory.

The record attendance for a Derby fixture at Pride Park was set during the 1999/2000 Premier League season when 33,758 witnessed the Rams face Liverpool on 18 March 2000. Meanwhile back at the Baseball Ground, a whopping 41,826 packed into witness a First Division clash with Tottenham Hotspur on 20 September 1969.

YOUNGEST PLAYER

Academy graduate Mason Bennett currently holds the record as Derby County's youngest player. The current Millwall forward was aged just 15 years and 99 days old when he made his Rams' debut in a Championship fixture away to Middlesbrough on 22 October 2011.

Bennett also holds the record of being the club's youngest goalscorer having netted his first Rams' goal in an FA Cup tie against Tranmere Rovers on 5 January 2013 aged 16 years 174 days.

SQUAD
2021/22

16 RICHARD STEARMAN

POSITION: Defender

DOB: 19/08/1987

COUNTRY: England

Central defender Richard Stearman trained with the Rams in pre-season as a free agent and agreed a one-year deal at Pride Park on the eve of the new 2021/22 season.

A vastly-experienced performer at Championship level, 34-year-old Stearman has amassed almost 450 career appearances having begun his career with Leicester City and taken in spells with Wolverhampton Wanderers, Ipswich Town, Fulham, Sheffield United and Huddersfield Town.

17 LOUIE SIBLEY

POSITION: Midfielder

DOB: 13/09/2001

COUNTRY: England

England U19 international Louie Sibley has been with the Rams since joining the club's Academy at U8 level. The 2021/22 season will be the attack-minded midfielder's second season as a professional having already made 49 first-team appearances and scored six goals before the new campaign got underway.

Sibley showed exactly what he is capable of when he curled home a tremendous late equaliser against promotion-seeking Brentford last season and Rams fans will be hopeful of seeing more of the same in 2021/22.

21 KELLE ROOS

POSITION: Goalkeeper

DOB: 31/05/1992

COUNTRY: Netherlands

Attempting to try and dislodge Scotland international David Marshall from the No1 spot at Pride Park has been a tough challenge for goalkeeper Kelle Roos.

The 2020/21 season saw the 29-year-old Dutch stopper deputise for Marshall in times of injury or illness and he then finished the campaign as first choice when the Rams secured their Championship status on the final day of the season.

26 LEE BUCHANAN

POSITION: Defender

DOB: 07/03/2001

COUNTRY: England

One of a great crop of youngsters who has progressed from the club's Academy to the first team, left-sided defender Lee Buchanan made 37 first-team appearances in all competitions for the Rams last season.

The Mansfield-born defender, who turns 21 in March, saw his development in 2020/21 rewarded with the Sammy Crooks Young Player of the Year award after his clean tackling and comfort on the ball won him many admirers.

IMPOSSIBLE
Footy Decisions

Would you rather...

have to play the rest of your football games in 35 degree heat or a blizzard?

Would you rather...

have Tom Lawrence's ability to score goals or Kelle Roos' ability to save them?

Would you rather...

have a pause button or a rewind button for your life?

Would you rather...

have unlimited battery life on all your devices or free wifi wherever you go?

Would you rather...

run 100 laps of the pitch or complete 200 burpees?

Would you rather...

Score the FA Cup final winning goal against Forest in your only game for Derby County or play 300 games for the Rams in League One?

Would you rather...

be remembered for a terrible footy howler or be forgotten completely?

Would you rather...

sell your best player to Nottingham Forest for £50m or sell him abroad for £20m?

Would you rather...

have to take a penalty against Kelle Roos or have Sam Baldock take a penalty against you?

Would you rather...

sit right at the back during a game or have the best seats in the stadium, but not be allowed to eat, drink or use the bathroom?

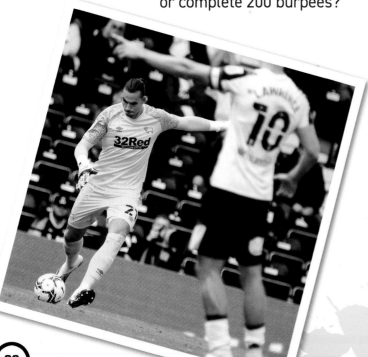

Would you rather...

be the star in league Two
Or a squad player
in the Premier League?

Would you rather...

Derby County win the FA Cup
or England win the World Cup?

Would you rather...

your match superstition be wearing
the same socks for a season Or the
same underwear for a month?

Would you rather...

**lose on television or
win with nobody watching?**

Would you rather...

have a long, average playing career or have
a short, fantastic career cut short by injury?

Would you rather...

lose to Forest twice
and finish top or beat them
twice and finish bottom?

Would you rather...

**clean the dressing room
toilet with your toothbrush
or the floor with your tongue?**

Would you rather...

play only five minutes
for the Rams or win
the Premier League
with Forest?

Would you rather...

have to wear every shirt inside out
or every pair of pants backwards?

Would you rather...

give up your mobile phone for
a month or bathing for a month?

Would you rather...

be alone all your life or surrounded
by Nottingham Forest supporters?

Would you rather...

play for Derby
County and always
lose or sit on the
bench and the Rams
always win?

Would you rather...

the half-time menu got rid of pies or pop?

Would you rather...

become a legendary manager
or a legendary player?

39

NATHAN
BYRNE

Derby County paid a then British record £225,000 to Leicester City when they signed left-back David Nish in August 1972. Signed by Brian Clough, Nish featured in the Rams' 1972/73 European Cup adventure and he later became a star performer under the guidance of new manager Dave Mackay.

Nish played a vital role in helping the Rams secure their second First Division title triumph in 1974/75 and was also a Charity Shield winner in August 1975. Such was his club form at the Baseball Ground that he won five England caps as a Derby player. David played a total of 237 games for Derby and scored 14 goals between 1972 and 1978.

RAMS HEROES

DAVID NISH

TEMPERAMENT

Often faced with containing tricky wingers, David Nish had the perfect mindset for defending. He very rarely lost concentration and always kept his cool. In the heat of any on-field duel, Nish kept his mind on the task in hand and more often than not came out on top in one-on-one situations.

RALLYING CALL

An experienced player and England international, Nish's ability to lead and inspire his teammates was there for all to see. Always there with an encouraging call to those around him, David led by example and was never afraid to let players know if standards had dropped.

QUICK ON HIS HEELS

Nish was always alive and alert to danger and when it occurred he was quick on his heels to track and tackle opponents. Not only was he swift over the ground but he was also quick to leap and win headed duels too.

PASSING SKILLS

Always comfortable with the ball at his feet, David was an accomplished ball-playing full-back who could always be relied upon to bring the ball out of defence and help the side turn defence to attack.

41

2006/07

The 2006/07 campaign was the second successive season that Spanish kit manufacturer Joma produced the Rams' playing kit. The white v-necked shirt had a thin line of black piping on the front which led to a black panel on the shoulder area while the top section of the collar was also black. The club crest sat in the centre of the shirt with the manufacturer's logo above and sponsor's branding below.

The black shorts had white side panels and carried both the Joma logo and club crest. The black and white socks had the manufacturer's name on the front.

DRESSED TO IMPRESS

Battling for promotion to the Premier League throughout the 2006/07 season, Derby fell just short of the top two spots but produced a successful Play-Off campaign to secure promotion.

The Rams defeated Southampton in an epic Play-Off semi-final before overcoming West Bromwich Albion in the Wembley final. The team did wear a one-off special kit for the final.

HE WORE IT WELL

After joining the Rams in January 2007 following a £750,000 switch from Motherwell, Stephen Pearson proved to be Derby County's promotion-winning hero.

Pearson lit up the rain-soaked Play-Off final match with West Bromwich Albion when he struck the only goal of the game after 61 minutes. The goal sealed promotion to the Premier League as the Rams finally ended their Play-Off hoodoo at the fourth time of asking.

Stylish Italian sports manufacturer Kappa produced a real Derby County classic for the 2013/14 season. The plain white shirt had a bold, black v-neck collar and a black band on the sleeves.

A very simple but effective design, the shirt also had the Kappa logo on each sleeve plus the manufacturer's name, club crest and sponsor's logo on the chest area.

The all-back shorts were decorated with the Kappa logo on each side plus the club crest and manufacturer's name on the front. An all-white sock was topped with a black band with a white Ram motif while the Kappa branding was in black on the shin pad area.

DRESSED TO IMPRESS

A seven-match winning run at the end of 2013 propelled Steve McClaren's men right into the 2013/14 Championship promotion picture.

Chasing down runaway leaders Leicester City and Burnley, the Rams ended the season third on 85 points. After dispatching Brighton & Hove Albion in the Play-Off semi-finals, the Rams sadly faltered at the final hurdle when they narrowly lost the final to QPR at Wembley.

HE WORE IT WELL

Striker Chris Martin certainly looked the part in the Rams' 2013/14 kit – the Scotland international scored 25 goals in all competitions to lead the scoring charts at Pride Park.

Of Martin's 25-goal haul, 20 came in the Championship's regulation season before he then scored a goal in each leg of the Play-Off semi-final games with Brighton.

2013/14

ALL KITTED OUT

SQUAD

2021/22

31 RYAN ALLSOP

POSITION: Goalkeeper

DOB: 17/06/1992

COUNTRY: England

A key member of the Wycombe Wanderers side that won promotion to the Championship in 2019/20, much-travelled goalkeeper Ryan Allsop ended a three-year stint at Adams Park when he signed a one-year deal with the Rams in August 2021.

A former England youth international, Allsop gained Premier League experience during his five-season spell at AFC Bournemouth. His arrival at Pride Park will certainly create healthy competition for the No1 position at Derby County.

32 JORDAN BROWN

POSITION: Defender / Midfielder

DOB: 21/06/2001

COUNTRY: England

With great composure on the ball, 20-year-old Academy graduate Jordan Brown has the ability to play anywhere across the backline or in a central midfield role.

Following a series of impressive displays at U18 and U23 level, Brown stepped up to train with the first team at the end of the 2019/20 campaign and made his debut as a substitute away to West Bromwich Albion in July 2020. In the opening weeks of the new 2021/22 season he featured in both of the Rams' EFL Cup fixtures.

33 CURTIS DAVIES

POSITION: Defender

DOB: 15/03/1985

COUNTRY: England

Veteran defender Curtis Davies brings a plethora of experience and know-how to the Derby Country squad having played over 500 professional games, primarily at Championship and Premier League level.

The 36-year-old is a great influence on the younger members of the squad and a real role model for the youthful crop of defenders on the books at Pride Park. He made 14 first-team appearances in 2020/21.

34 JACK STRETTON

POSITION: Striker

DOB: 06/09/2001

COUNTRY: Scotland

Young forward Jack Stretton has progressed through the Rams' Academy and appears to have a bright future ahead of him after producing a number of performances that caught the eye of manager Wayne Rooney.

The 2020/21 season was Stretton's first as a professional and after scoring eight goals in eight games for the U23 team he was given a first-team debut as a substitute against Wycombe Wanderers in November 2020. He made three further first-team appearances last season and will be looking to continue his involvement in Rooney's plans in 2021/22.

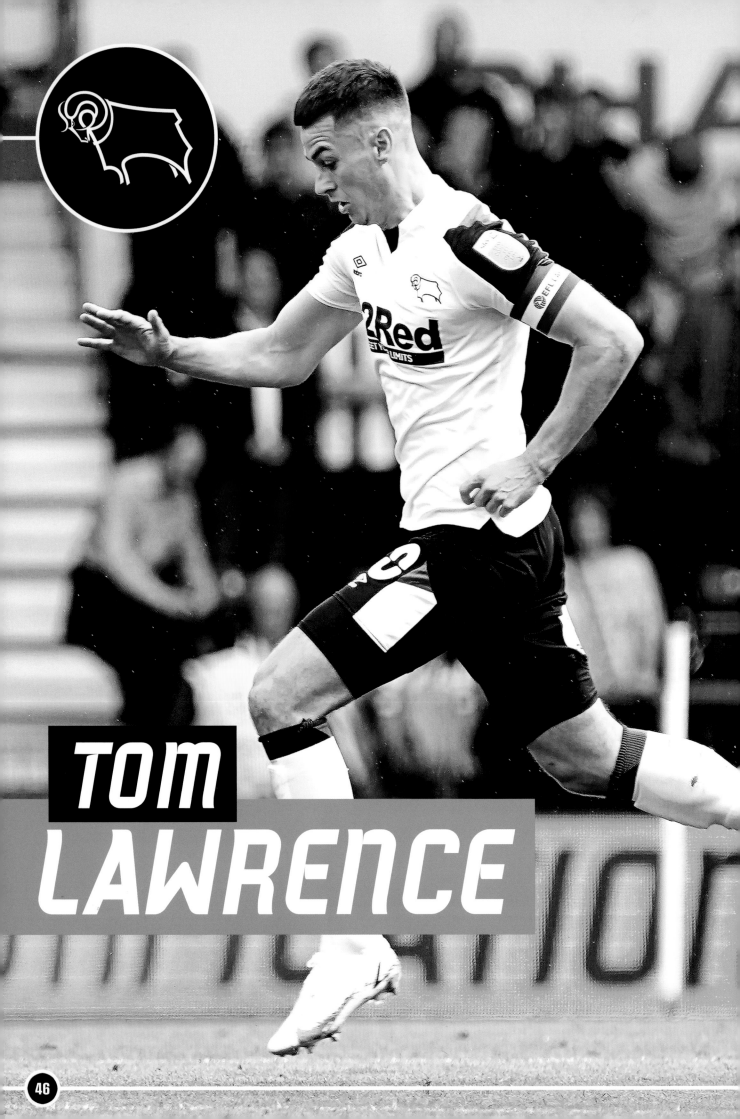

TOM
LAWRENCE

One of a player's greatest assets is the ability to win the ball. The following exercise can be used to improve a player's tackling abilities.

TACKLING

SOCCER SKILLS

EXERCISE

Set up a 10m x 20m grid.

In this two-on-two exercise, the aim of the game is to score a goal by taking the ball past the two opposing defenders, to the end line, and stand on the ball. The defenders just have to stop them.

As well as producing plenty of opportunities for the defenders to tackle, this session will test the defenders' abilities to work together, and communicate.

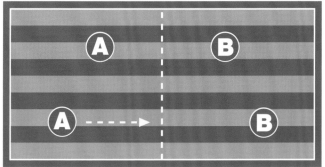

Key Factors

1. Be patient - do not dive in.

2. Stay on your feet if possible.

3. Time the tackle with bodyweight behind it.

4. Be determined to win it.

The reason that great players win so many tackles is not just because they know how to tackle and have good technique, it is because they have big hearts and are determined to win their challenges on the pitch.

ODD BALLS

1

C
B
D
A
ANSWER

2

B
A
C
D
1898
ANSWER

Three of the four pictures in each football represent a Premier League or EFL club, can you figure out the football club as well as the odd one out?

3

C
B
A
D
ANSWER

4

C
B
D
A
FOOTBALL CLUB
ANSWER

5

B
A
C
D
ANSWER

PLAYER
OF THE YEAR

GRAEME SHINNIE

Derby County's supporters voted Graeme Shinnie as their 2020/21 Player of the Season. The midfielder landed the prestigious Jack Stamps award following a voting poll on the club's official website. The 29-year-old Scotsman was a regular in the Derby side throughout the campaign and he racked up 43 appearances in all competitions, with only Jason Knight and Matt Clarke appearing on more occasions.

Shinnie also found the back of the net three times in the Rams' Sky Bet Championship campaign and his goals proved something of a lucky omen - Derby never suffered defeat in the games he scored in.

Two of the Scotland international's goals came from the penalty-spot in the vital victories over Birmingham City in December and Luton Town in April.

His other goal came in Derby's 1-1 draw at promotion-chasing AFC Bournemouth at the end of October.

Shinnie's wholehearted and never-say-die displays in the middle of the park made him a regular in the starting line-up during the season and especially under Wayne Rooney after he took over as manager towards the end of 2020.

He also wore the captain's armband in the closing weeks of the season, demonstrating his natural leadership skills having fulfilled the same role at his previous clubs, as Rooney's side preserved their Championship status for the 2021/22 campaign.

Shinnie, who began his career at Inverness Caledonian Thistle in Scotland, joined the Rams from Aberdeen in the summer of 2019. A consistent performer in a Derby County shirt, he had made 70 appearances and scored five goals for the club as at the end of the 2020/21 campaign.

YOUNG PLAYER OF THE SEASON
LEE BUCHANAN

Left-back Lee Buchanan took the honour of being named as Derby County's Sammy Crooks Young Player of the Season for 2020/21. The Academy graduate enjoyed a progressive personal season as he established himself as a first-team regular after making his debut in the previous campaign.

He made 37 appearances in total across the 2020/21 season and his performances were rewarded with a call-up to the England U21 side for the first time in November 2020.

The defender racked up over 2,500 minutes of match action in the Sky Bet Championship over the course of 2020/21, while he also registered three assists going forward. With approaching 50 first-team outings to his name, a great deal will be expected of Buchanan in 2021/22 as he continues his rapid progress with the Rams.

GRAEME
SHINNIE

COLOUR
KAMIL
JOZWIAK

35 LOUIE WATSON

POSITION: Midfielder

DOB: 06/07/2001

COUNTRY: Republic of Ireland

Midfielder Louie Watson joined Derby County from the West Ham United Academy in 2020 and broke into the first team in his debut season at Pride Park.

Watson was swiftly elevated from the U23 side to the first team and made his debut in the Rams' convincing 4-0 victory over Birmingham City in December 2020. He went on to feature in a further eight Championship fixtures and was handed a first start at home to Brentford in March 2021.

36 FESTY EBOSELE

POSITION: Defender

DOB: 02/08/2002

COUNTRY: Republic of Ireland

Now in his second season as a professional at Pride Park, pacy defender Festy Ebosele made his first-team debut in the closing weeks of the 2020/21 season.

A right-back who has great attacking intentions, the Republic of Ireland Youth international has all the attributes of the modern-day full-back. He continued his first team development with a substitute appearance in the opening-day draw with Huddersfield Town.

SQUAD
2021/22

POSITION: Defender

DOB: 01/10/2001

COUNTRY: England

The 2020/21 campaign saw Academy graduate Kornell McDonald force his way into Wayne Rooney's plans. He began the campaign in the U23 development squad but impressed Rooney and the club's coaching staff when training with the first-team squad.

The teenager made his first-team debut in the Rams' goalless draw away to Brentford when he replaced the injured Curtis Davies. He was handed a first start when Derby hosted champions-elect, Norwich City in April 2021.

POSITION: Midfielder

DOB: 13/02/2001

COUNTRY: Republic of Ireland

An energetic and exciting midfielder, Jason Knight is another home-grown hero to emerge from the club's Academy.

Knight was given his first taste of professional football when he debuted in the Rams' opening game of the 2019/20 campaign. A Republic of Ireland U21 international, he featured in 45 first-team fixtures last season and chipped in with three goals.

1. WHO AM I?

I arrived at Derby in March 1997

My previous club was Portsmouth

My debut coincided with a memorable 3-2 win over Manchester United at Old Trafford

Supporters voted me the club's Player of the Season in 1999/2000

After 146 league games for the Rams I moved on to Sunderland

3. WHO AM I?

I began my career with the Rams

I made my Derby debut against Peterborough United

I won international recognition with England at U21 level while at Pride Park

In 2012/13 I won the club's Sammy Crooks Young Player of the Year award

I have since left Derby and am now plying my trade in the Premier League

GUESS WHO

2. WHO AM I?

I was born in Stockport in 1992

I began my career at Liverpool

I was voted the Football League's Young Player of the Year in 2012/13

I initially came to Derby on loan before signing permanently

My father was an England international

I was born in Wrexham in 1974

I made my league debut for Crewe Alexandra

I joined Derby in a £1.5M deal in January 2008

I made 135 appearances for Derby and scored seven goals

I am now a well known pundit on television and radio

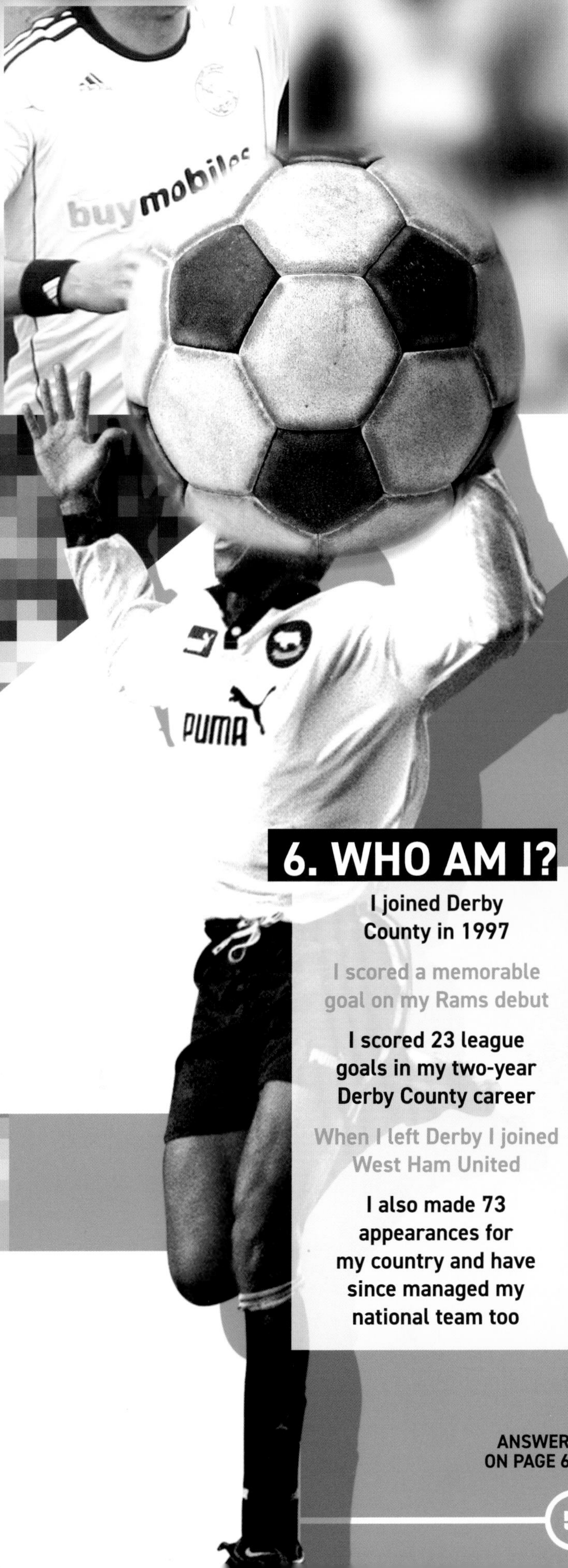

Can you identify these six Rams from the clues given? Good luck!

4. WHO AM I?

I began my professional career with Norwich City

I enjoyed Wembley success while on loan at Luton Town

I first came to Pride Park on loan but later joined permanently

I was on target in the 2014 Play-Off semi-final victory over Brighton & Hove Albion which took the Rams to Wembley

I am currently playing for a Championship rival

5. WHO AM I?

6. WHO AM I?

I joined Derby County in 1997

I scored a memorable goal on my Rams debut

I scored 23 league goals in my two-year Derby County career

When I left Derby I joined West Ham United

I also made 73 appearances for my country and have since managed my national team too

ANSWERS ON PAGE 62

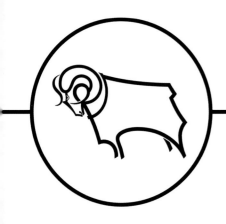

Italian international Stefano Eranio joined Derby County from AC Milan in May 1997 and proved to be one of Jim Smith's most influential signings. Famed for netting the club's first goal at Pride Park and being named in the Rams' greatest-ever team, Eranio was a firm fans' favourite.

He made 108 appearances for Derby, scoring ten goals, between 1997 and 2001. He also won 20 caps for Italy. A skilful and creative player, who operated mainly on the right side of midfield, Eranio was highly respected by teammates and the club's supporters who viewed him as one of the Rams' most influential players of the modern era.

RAMS HEROES

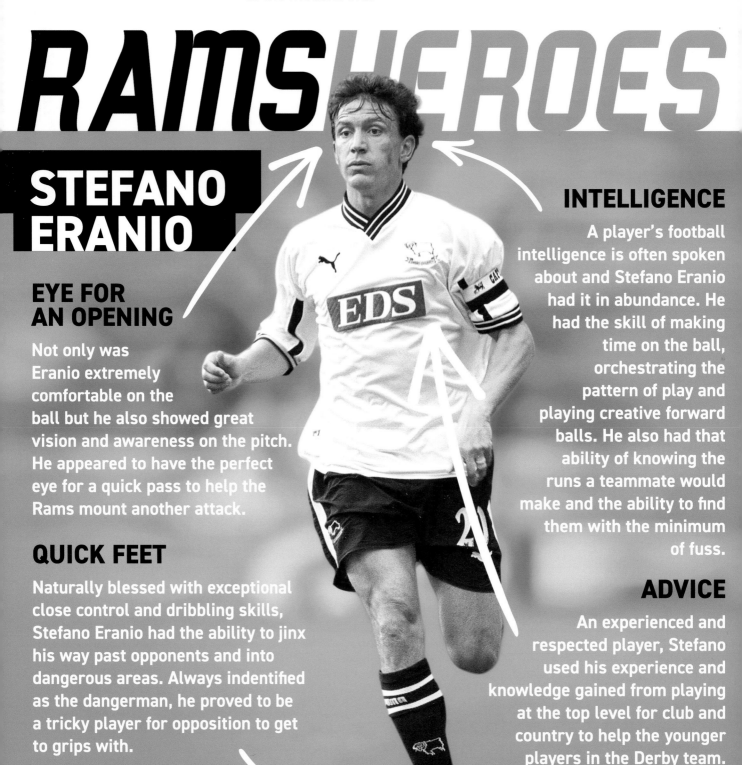

STEFANO ERANIO

INTELLIGENCE

A player's football intelligence is often spoken about and Stefano Eranio had it in abundance. He had the skill of making time on the ball, orchestrating the pattern of play and playing creative forward balls. He also had that ability of knowing the runs a teammate would make and the ability to find them with the minimum of fuss.

EYE FOR AN OPENING

Not only was Eranio extremely comfortable on the ball but he also showed great vision and awareness on the pitch. He appeared to have the perfect eye for a quick pass to help the Rams mount another attack.

QUICK FEET

Naturally blessed with exceptional close control and dribbling skills, Stefano Eranio had the ability to jinx his way past opponents and into dangerous areas. Always indentified as the dangerman, he proved to be a tricky player for opposition to get to grips with.

ADVICE

An experienced and respected player, Stefano used his experience and knowledge gained from playing at the top level for club and country to help the younger players in the Derby team.

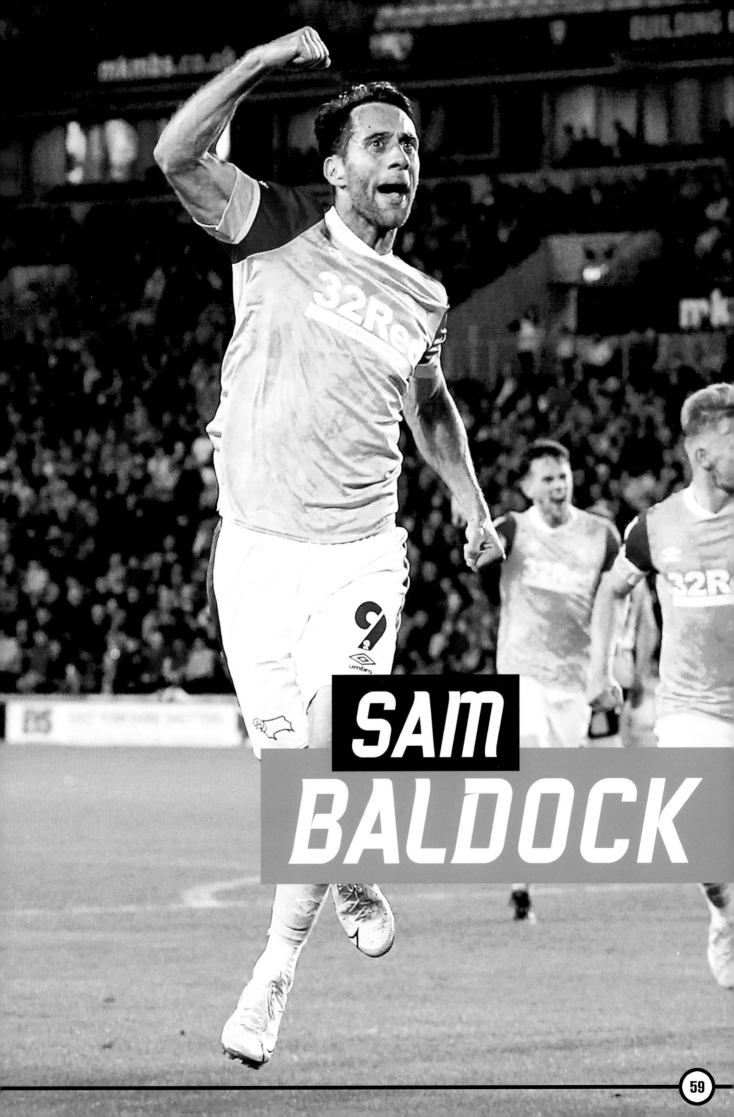

SAM
BALDOCK

FAST FORWARD>>

Do your predictions for 2021/22 match our own?

CHAMPIONSHIP WINNERS

Derby County

CHAMPIONSHIP TOP SCORER

Sam Baldock

CHAMPIONSHIP RUNNERS-UP

Fulham

CHAMPIONSHIP PLAY-OFF WINNERS

Reading

FA CUP WINNERS

Brighton & Hove Albion

FA CUP RUNNERS-UP

Leeds United

LEAGUE CUP WINNERS

Arsenal

LEAGUE CUP RUNNERS-UP

Watford

PREMIER LEAGUE WINNERS
Manchester United

PREMIER LEAGUE RUNNERS-UP
Chelsea

PREMIER LEAGUE TOP SCORER
Anthony Martial

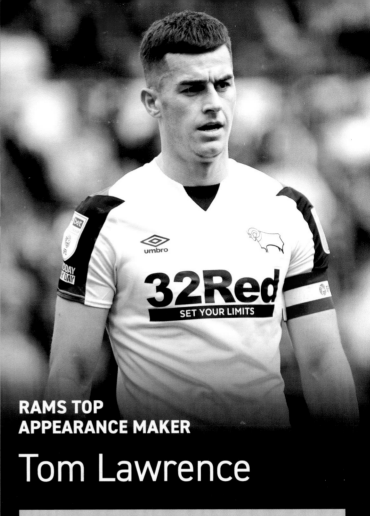

RAMS TOP APPEARANCE MAKER
Tom Lawrence

RAMS PLAYER OF THE YEAR
Colin Kazim-Richards

CHAMPIONS LEAGUE WINNERS
Barcelona

CHAMPIONS LEAGUE RUNNERS-UP
Real Madrid

EUROPA LEAGUE WINNERS
West Ham United

EUROPA LEAGUE RUNNERS-UP
Lazio

ANSWERS

PAGE 11
SOCCER SEARCH

Bicycle Kick.

PAGE 14
CLASSIC FANTASTIC

PAGE 26
GUESS THE CLUB

1. Newcastle United. 2. Wigan Athletic. 3. Leeds United.
4. Charlton Athletic. 5. Coventry City. 6. AFC Wimbledon.
7. Stoke City. 8. Millwall. 9.Wolverhampton Wanderers.
10. Nottingham Forest.

PAGE 48
ODD BALLS

1. Sunderland, C. 2. Portsmouth, C. 3. Arsenal, B.
4. Crewe Alexandra, A. 5. Queens Park Rangers, C.
6. Crystal Palace, B. 7. Blackburn Rovers, B.
8. Reading, B. 9. Birmingham City, C.
10. West Ham United, D.

PAGE 56
GUESS WHO?

1. Mart Poom. 2. Tom Ince. 3. Will Hughes.
4. Robbie Savage. 5. Chris Martin. 6. Paulo Wanchope.